Original title:
Laughter Across Horizons

Copyright © 2025 Swan Charm
All rights reserved.

Author: Kätriin Kaldaru
ISBN HARDBACK: 978-9908-1-3304-1
ISBN PAPERBACK: 978-9908-1-3305-8
ISBN EBOOK: 978-9908-1-3306-5

The Smile that Travels

Across the miles, a smile glows,
Bringing warmth where'er it goes.
A bridge of joy, a spark so bright,
Connecting souls, igniting light.

In every heart, it plants a seed,
A gentle touch, a quiet deed.
Through laughter's echo, hopes take flight,
A shared embrace, a pure delight.

Waves of Amusement

The ocean laughs with playful waves,
Inviting joy that nature saves.
Each ripple dances, leaps, and sways,
In sunlit afternoons of praise.

Children squeal, their spirits free,
As seagulls join in harmony.
The tide of mirth, a soothing balm,
In every splash, a moment calm.

Fables of Cheer in Distant Lands

In lands afar, where stories twine,
Cheerful fables brightly shine.
Adventures told 'neath starlit skies,
With laughter shared, the heart complies.

From whispered tales of daring feats,
To merry songs on bustling streets.
Each circle made around the fire,
Ignites the soul with joy and desire.

Radiant Tides of Fun

With every wave, the laughter swells,
In radiant tides, enchantment dwells.
Children play as sunbeams dance,
In moments flushed with pure romance.

The world ignites with vibrant hues,
As smiles bouquet in joyful views.
In every splash, in every cheer,
The tide of fun is ever near.

Distant Echoes of Delight

Whispers of laughter float on the breeze,
Memories dance under the swaying trees.
Sunsets painted in gold and in pink,
Moments of joy that make our hearts sink.

Joyful echoes of days gone by,
As twilight settles, and stars touch the sky.
Dreams once spoken, now silent and sweet,
In the stillness, our pasts gently meet.

Footsteps retraced on familiar ground,
Footprints of sunshine where love once found.
In the distance, a melody plays,
A tune of enchantment that forever stays.

Each sound a reminder of warmth and bliss,
A promise of laughter, a lingering kiss.
The heart holds the tales that time cannot steal,
In echoes of joy, we eternally heal.

With every whisper, the night comes alive,
In the warmth of our memories, we thrive.
Distant echoes weave stories so bright,
Guiding us home through the velvet night.

The Odyssey of Radiant Mirth

Through valleys of laughter, we journey anew,
With each step forward, our spirits renew.
Bright smiles like sunshine, radiate cheer,
In the heart of adventure, we conquer our fear.

The path is adventures, where giggles arise,
With each twist and turn, there's joy in disguise.
Every heartbeat a rhythm that dances with glee,
In the moments we cherish, we feel truly free.

Stars glisten like lanterns in the velvet so deep,
As we wander through dreams that never shall sleep.
Stories of friendship, stitched into the night,
Our odyssey sparkles, an infinite flight.

Echoes of laughter ring out in the sky,
As we soar like kite strings, so daringly high.
In the tapestry woven from whimsy and fun,
Our radiant mirth shines brightly as one.

With hearts intertwined and hands all aglow,
We embrace the adventures wherever we go.
The odyssey flows in the waves of delight,
As we paint the horizon with colors so bright.

Whimsical Ramblings Under Bright Skies

Under bright skies, we wander along,
With dreams in our hearts and a whimsical song.
Nature's embrace in every soft breeze,
We dance in the sunshine beneath swaying trees.

Thoughts drift like clouds, both gentle and grand,
With laughter that twinkles like grains of sand.
In the realm of our minds, we let spirits fly,
Embracing the magic that brightens the sky.

Butterflies flutter in a shimmering dance,
Drawing us closer to life's sweet romance.
Every moment's a treasure, a gift from above,
In whimsical ramblings, we find endless love.

The colors of joy paint our world anew,
A canvas of wonder, forever in view.
With each passing hour, our hearts come alive,
In the ease of the day, our dreams freely thrive.

So, let's chase the sunlight and laugh till we fall,
With spirits unbound, we can conquer it all.
Under bright skies, we shall forever reside,
In whimsical ramblings, with hearts open wide.

Ripples of Smiles in the Sun

In golden light, we share our glee,
Laughter dances, wild and free.
Children playing, shadows weave,
Nature whispers, hearts believe.

Every moment, joy unfolds,
Hand in hand, warmth it holds.
Ripples spark in sparkling streams,
Life's delight shines in our dreams.

Sun-kissed laughter fills the air,
We find magic everywhere.
A simple glance, a knowing nod,
In this moment, we applaud.

Let the smiles with colors blend,
Time stands still, on smiles depend.
An echo of the love we find,
In ripples, hearts are intertwined.

A Symphony of Cheerful Stories

The sun awakes with golden beams,
A tale begins in cheerful dreams.
Each note a laugh, each beat a smile,
In this symphony, stay awhile.

Voices rise like birds in flight,
Stories weave through day and night.
In every word, joy dances free,
A melody of harmony.

From whispered hopes to shouts of cheer,
Together we bring stories near.
Our laughter echoes, soft and true,
A symphony, just me and you.

Let hearts collide, let spirits play,
In cheerful stories, we find our way.
A world adorned with vibrant hues,
In this symphony, we sing our truths.

Sunkissed Smirks Journeying On

A day awakes with a warm embrace,
Sunkissed smirks on every face.
We wander paths, our spirits light,
In laughter's glow, the world feels right.

With every step, the sun does beam,
A journey comes alive, a dream.
Side by side, we share the fun,
A dance of joy beneath the sun.

In gentle breezes, whispers play,
Collecting smiles along the way.
With every glance, connections grow,
In fondness, we let our hearts glow.

Time may pass, but bonds remain,
Our sunkissed smirks, a sweet refrain.
With every memory, we carry on,
A journey bright, forever drawn.

The Celebration of Joyful Affections

Gather 'round, let voices soar,
In joyful affections, we explore.
A celebration, hearts aglow,
In warmth and laughter, love will flow.

We dance beneath the twinkling stars,
With open arms, no need for bars.
Embraces weave a tapestry,
In every glance, shared history.

The joy we find in every face,
A tender touch, a warm embrace.
With every heartbeat, love's sweet tune,
We celebrate beneath the moon.

In moments shared, we come alive,
With joyful affections, we thrive.
Together, we write a story fine,
In love's pure glow, forever shine.

Whispers of Cheer Traveling Far

In the breeze, laughter flows,
Carried on wings of the sun,
Every smile a tale bestows,
Joyful journeys just begun.

Whispers dance on the air,
Sowing seeds of delight,
Hearts entwined everywhere,
Shining in soft twilight.

Through valleys and over hills,
Happiness finds its way,
With every heart that thrills,
Bright colors of the day.

Footsteps tracing the ground,
Echoes of laughter shared,
Sweet moments all around,
In each soul, joy declared.

Far away yet so near,
Connections rise like dawn,
In the whispers we hear,
Cheerful dreams to lean on.

Unruly Moods of Faraway Places

Desert storms rage and fight,
Moods shift like quicksand's grip,
In shadows and in light,
Travelers' hearts do flip.

Rainforest secrets brew,
Glimmers of laughter's sound,
Thoughts swirl like morning dew,
In faraway lands, unbound.

Mountain peaks with a frown,
Snowflakes tinged with despair,
Yet joy can still be found,
In skies beyond compare.

Cities pulse, a wild beat,
Colors clash without pause,
Every stranger we meet,
Can turn our heads and jaws.

In markets filled with dreams,
Chaos shapes the day bright,
Life's tapestry, it seems,
Holds every shade of light.

Celestial Notes of Amusement

Stars twinkle, soft and bright,
Playing tunes on night's skin,
Whispers of cosmic delight,
Inviting all to join in.

Planets waltz through the sky,
Chasing comets so fleet,
With every glimmering sigh,
Euphoria can't be beat.

Galaxies spin and sway,
In the universe's dance,
Every note finds its way,
In the ethereal trance.

Meteor showers race by,
Wishes dart, hope takes flight,
Holding dreams in the sky,
In the sweet, starry night.

Celestial laughter sings,
Echoed in cosmic space,
Where joy's light truly clings,
And time finds a gentle pace.

Trails of Joy that Never End

Paths woven with delight,
Where every step brings cheer,
Sunrise to meet the night,
On trails we hold so dear.

Flowers bloom with great flair,
Scents of laughter arise,
In the breeze, love's soft air,
Each moment filled with skies.

Winding roads lead us on,
Through forests lush and green,
With every dusk and dawn,
The joy stays evergreen.

The mountains call our name,
Their peaks touch the divine,
In nature's endless game,
We find our hearts align.

So let's dance on these ways,
In harmony, we blend,
For life's bright, shining rays,
Are trails that never end.

Revelry Beneath Expansive Skies

Under the wide, endless dome,
Joyous laughter begins to roam.
Colors dance in vibrant light,
Hearts uplifted, spirits bright.

Bubbles float, dreams take flight,
Voices blend in pure delight.
All around, a sweet refrain,
Echoes softly, like the rain.

Friends gather close, hands entwined,
In this moment, love defined.
Stars above, a sparkling show,
Together we will brightly glow.

Fireflies twinkle, whispers sweet,
In this magic, life is fleet.
Laughter's cradle, time will bend,
Here in joy, there is no end.

As shadows lengthen, we will stay,
In the bliss of this grand play.
Under skies so vast and free,
We find our place, just you and me.

Tickles of Cheer from Faraway Lands

Winds carry whispers of delight,
From distant shores, they take their flight.
Each note dances, a gentle tease,
Filling hearts with sweet unease.

Market stalls with colors bright,
Fragrant spices, pure delight.
Songs of laughter, tales of yore,
Eager souls that seek much more.

Together we explore the sights,
Underneath a canopy of nights.
Each heartbeat sings a different tune,
Beneath the glow of a silver moon.

Exotic dances, lively sway,
Culture shared in joyful play.
In this realm of vibrant dreams,
Life is stitched with joyful seams.

The world spins in a wondrous arc,
Filling hearts with a glowing spark.
Each adventure, memories grand,
Tickles of cheer from far-off land.

Cackles and Cries Beneath the Same Sun

In the warmth of the blazing light,
Cackles echo with pure delight.
Children play with carefree glee,
While nature hums a symphony.

Voices rise, a joyous sound,
Across the hills, they bounce around.
Laughter mingles with the breeze,
In the dance of swaying trees.

As the sun sets, colors blend,
A tapestry that never ends.
Cackles and cries, a summer's tune,
Underneath the watchful moon.

Evening whispers, stories shared,
In this moment, hearts have dared.
To love, to laugh, beneath the sun,
We are together, joined as one.

And as night falls, stars appear,
Guiding us with what we hold dear.
Cackles and cries, their echo stays,
In the light of our joyful days.

Uplifted Spirits in the Open Air

Fresh breezes dance, a gentle sigh,
Underneath the endless sky.
Feet in grass, we sway and spin,
Breath of freedom, let joy begin.

Clouds drift softly, tales unfold,
Stories of wonder yet untold.
In every heartbeat, in each laugh,
We find connection's warming path.

Above, the birds, they spread their wings,
Chasing dreams, as freedom sings.
Joy in motion, wild and free,
Uplifted spirits, you and me.

The beauty blooms in every glance,
Bearing witness to this dance.
In open air, we feel the rush,
United by this vibrant hush.

As twilight falls and shadows play,
Evening whispers of the day.
Hearts we raise like kites in flight,
In the open air, we find our light.

Celestial Laughs from Afar

Stars twinkle bright in the night,
Sharing secrets with the moonlight.
In whispers soft, they dance and play,
Casting shadows of dreams that sway.

Galaxies spin in joyful spree,
Laughter echoing, wild and free.
Each comet's tail a bright delight,
Filling hearts with magical light.

Nebulae paint the sky in hues,
Of vibrant joy, in reds and blues.
While planets hum a gentle tune,
Cradled within the arms of June.

Through the cosmos, chuckles fly,
Bouncing off the asteroids nearby.
In the silence, joy takes flight,
In celestial laughs, day turns to night.

So look above when skies are clear,
And find the laughter waiting here.
For in the vastness, you will see,
The universe laughs in harmony.

A Voyage Through Jest

Set sail on waves of cheerful jest,
With laughter guiding, it's the best.
Each ripple tells a tale of cheer,
Whispers of joy that draw us near.

The sails are filled with giggles bright,
As sunbeams dance, casting their light.
We navigate through smiles and fun,
Chasing happiness till the day is done.

Between the clouds, the humor flows,
In breezy gusts, our friendship grows.
With every wave, our spirits rise,
Adventurous hearts, in laughter, wise.

The horizon calls with jokes untold,
In the playful winds, we are bold.
For every jest and playful tease,
Brings forth a warmth, a gentle ease.

Anchor down, in the harbor of glee,
We've traveled far, just you and me.
In the end, it's love we invest,
Through every adventure and joyful jest.

Aurora of Amusement

Dawn breaks softly with a grin,
Painting the world, where laughs begin.
In hues of gold, and pinks so bright,
Awakening joy, sparking delight.

The sun stretches, yawns, and shares,
With morning dew, laughter repairs.
Nature dances, fresh and alive,
Wrapped in the joy that helps us thrive.

Every blossom bursts in cheer,
Swaying gently, drawing near.
Bees hum a melody so sweet,
As life orchestrates a grand heartbeat.

Clouds play coy, drifting so high,
Whispering jokes in the azure sky.
Each ray of warmth, a hug from above,
Spreading joy like an endless love.

In this aurora, we find our way,
Through paths of laughter, bright as day.
Embracing the beauty and charm we've spun,
In the tapestry of life, we are one.

The Essence of Joyful Paths

Winding trails through fields of green,
Where laughter echoes, soft and serene.
Footsteps light, on paths so wide,
In every heart, let joy reside.

Beneath the boughs of ancient trees,
We find the whispers of the breeze.
Each branch a story, each leaf a song,
In this joyful dance, we belong.

Through meadows blooming, spirits rise,
With every petal, joy multiplies.
Skip along to the rhythm of birds,
In nature's chorus, laughter heard.

Each twist and turn, new sights await,
Life's simple moments, intoxicating fate.
With every smile and every glance,
We weave together, love's romance.

Embrace the journey, cherish the cheer,
In the essence of joy, we persevere.
For on these paths, we truly see,
The beauty of life, in unity.

Joyful Footprints on Sandy Shores

Tiny toes in golden sand,
Leaving trails where dreams expand.
Laughter echoes with the tide,
Waves embrace, like arms open wide.

Sunset paints the sky so bright,
Colors dance in fading light.
Shells and treasures laid in line,
Nature's gifts, a pure design.

Seagulls cry, a cheerful song,
As we wander, time feels long.
Footprints traced in softest clay,
Memories made in splendid play.

Breezes whisper, secrets shared,
Moments cherished, hearts prepared.
From each step, there's joy and cheer,
On sandy shores, we hold what's dear.

As the night begins to fall,
Stars awaken, nature's call.
Hand in hand, we'll roam once more,
Together on the sandy shore.

Playful Shadows Cast by the Sun

Morning light breaks through the trees,
Dancing shadows on the breeze.
Shapes and forms that twist and glide,
As the sun begins to guide.

Kids are laughing, chasing dreams,
In the warmth of sunlight beams.
Every shadow, fun and bright,
Painting stories in the light.

Running wild with arms spread wide,
Joyful laughter, hearts abide.
In this game, we find our way,
Chasing shadows through the day.

As the sun dips, colors swirl,
Shadows dance in twilight's pearl.
Playful whispers in the night,
Memories held, forever bright.

With each sunset's gentle sigh,
We say goodbye, but not just lie.
In our hearts, the shadows stay,
Guiding us along the way.

The Dance of Whimsy and Wonder

A twirl of leaves in autumn's breeze,
Nature's laughter, joyous tease.
Branches sway, a playful song,
Inviting all to join along.

Stars above in nighttime's glow,
Lighting paths for dreams to flow.
Whispers soft, like secrets told,
Every moment, purest gold.

Dancing flowers in meadows wide,
Colors bloom, no need to hide.
In the wind, their laughter soars,
As they sway on open shores.

Giggling streams that run so free,
Reflecting all they wish to be.
Every ripple, every sound,
In this dance, our hearts are found.

Let us twirl through life's embrace,
With whimsy bright, we find our place.
In wonder's arms, we find our song,
Together, where our dreams belong.

Skylines of Chuckles

Above the city, laughter flies,
In every heart, a giggle lies.
Skyscrapers grin towards the skies,
Reflecting joy through playful eyes.

Breezes bring a cheerful sound,
As smiles bloom on every ground.
Bounding children chase the light,
Filling days with pure delight.

Twinkling lights like stars anew,
Sparkling dreams in evening's hue.
Laughter echoes, bright and clear,
A melody we hold so dear.

Street performers dance and sing,
Every note, a playful fling.
City's pulse, with beat and cheer,
Melodies that draw us near.

As the moon begins to rise,
Whispers drift, and laughter flies.
In this skyline, joy takes flight,
Living dreams in the night light.

Joyful Echoes of Distant Skies

In the morning light so fair,
Colors dance within the air.
Songs of laughter rise and swell,
Tales of joy we love to tell.

Clouds of silver drift and glide,
Hearts aflame, we laugh with pride.
In each breeze a memory flows,
Joyful echoes, love bestows.

Fields of green beneath the sun,
Every heartbeat, joy begun.
Nature sings in sweet embrace,
Everyone finds their own place.

As the sun begins to set,
Each bright moment, we won't regret.
In the twilight, stars appear,
Guiding dreams, dispelling fear.

Night's gentle touch brings us peace,
In its arms, all worries cease.
Sleep in harmony so deep,
Joyful echoes gently seep.

Chasing Giggles on the Wind

Laughter dances on the breeze,
Whispers play among the trees.
Children's giggles fill the air,
Joyful moments everywhere.

With each step, we chase the light,
Every shadow making bright.
Running wild, so free and bold,
Stories shared, both young and old.

Through the fields, we spin and twirl,
Dancing dreams in every whirl.
Chasing puddles, leaps we take,
Every giggle, hearts awake.

When the stars begin to shine,
Magic tingles, hearts align.
Underneath a moonlit sky,
Laughter echoes, sweet and spry.

So let joy be our true guide,
In each moment, smiles reside.
Chasing dreams, we revel on,
With each giggle, worries gone.

Whispers of Merriment in the Air

In the garden, laughter flies,
Whispers dance beneath the skies.
Every petal holds a cheer,
Echoing warmth that draws us near.

Sunlight sparkles on the stream,
Wishing well, we'd love to dream.
In the breeze, the joy ignites,
Twinkling like the stars at nights.

Games of chase, and happy screams,
Crafting bold and grander dreams.
Near the trees, kids play all day,
In their laughter, hearts will sway.

As the shadows stretch and sway,
We gather close, the end of day.
With every smile, a story shared,
In our hearts, the love declared.

So let us hold these precious ties,
Whispers linger in our sighs.
Merriment, a canvas bright,
Painting days with pure delight.

Smiles that Span the Seas

Across the waves, a tale unfolds,
Smiles that span both young and old.
With the tide, our laughter flows,
In every heart, the warmth it sows.

Sailing high on dreams we chase,
Adventures crafted, time and space.
In the sunset's golden hue,
Every smile is fresh and new.

Seagulls dance on ocean's breath,
Joyful spirits conquer death.
Together on this great expanse,
Found in every shared romance.

As we gather round the shore,
Waves of joy forevermore.
Holding close what truly lasts,
Fleeting moments turned to casts.

With the stars above, we see,
Smiles that span the mighty sea.
In each heart, a treasure gleams,
Together, we fulfill our dreams.

Wind-swept Tales of Joy

In fields of gold where laughter plays,
The breeze whispers secrets of sunny days.
Joy dances lightly on each gentle gust,
A song of freedom, an anthem of trust.

Children chase dreams where wildflowers bloom,
Their giggles echo like sweet, bright tunes.
Clouds drift above, painting skies so wide,
In nature's canvas, pure joy can't hide.

Beneath the trees where shadows embrace,
Laughter intertwines in a tender grace.
With every rustle, the world sings clear,
Wind-swept tales bring the heart close near.

Moments unfold like wings in flight,
As laughter spins in the soft twilight.
Life's simple wonders, a joy to behold,
In wind-swept tales, our stories unfold.

So carry this joy, let it freely flow,
Like whispers of wind in the warm, bright glow.
For in every tale, both humble and grand,
Lies the simple magic of love's gentle hand.

The Globe's Hidden Chortles

In corners of earth where shadows weave,
Laughter as light as a child's eave.
From bustling cities to quiet streams,
Hidden chortles weave hopes and dreams.

A child's giggle on a sunlit street,
Joy spills like rain, a rhythmic beat.
In every place where smiles are sown,
The world whispers secrets we have known.

Under the stars where the night is deep,
Laughter tickles the dreams we keep.
In every language, a chuckle is shared,
Echoes of joy show how much we cared.

Between the lines of life's grand review,
There lies a humor that feels so true.
In the silence, we find our song,
For hidden chortles play all along.

So wherever you roam, let laughter arise,
A global embrace under brightening skies.
In life's woven tapestry, warmth will unfurl,
The globe spins on laughter, a magical whirl.

Harmonies of Heartfelt Chuckles

In a crowded room, laughter ignites,
A chorus of chuckles that twinkles like lights.
Each smile a note in a joyful refrain,
Harmonies rise, erasing the pain.

Gathering moments like sweet, lingering sound,
Heartfelt chuckles, in friendship, abound.
With every shared story, we weave our song,
Together we flourish, where hearts all belong.

In whispers of hope and glances so bright,
Laughter is music in soft, warm light.
A melody crafted from trust and delight,
In heartfelt harmonies, our spirits take flight.

Through trials and triumphs, we sing and we play,
In laughter's embrace, we find our own way.
Each chuckle a blessing, each smile a gift,
In this symphony of life, we willingly lift.

So join in the song, let your heart be free,
In the rhythms of laughter, find joy's decree.
For harmonies flourish where love finds a spark,
In heartfelt chuckles, we light up the dark.

The Color of a Playful Heart

Brushstrokes of laughter paint the day,
In vibrant hues where dreams find their way.
The color of joy beams bright in the sun,
A playful heart knows life's just begun.

With each spirited dance, colors collide,
Whirling and twirling, the joy cannot hide.
Rainbows emerge from the simplest sparks,
In fields of imagination, free as larks.

In the laughter of children, a palette unfolds,
The warmth of their voices outshines the golds.
Each chuckle a brushstroke of heart's pure intent,
A kaleidoscope's charm, a moment well-spent.

So splash every canvas with laughter anew,
Let the dye of delight color skies bright and blue.
For life is a masterpiece, playful and bold,
In hues of our heart, the most beautiful gold.

Embrace every moment, let colors impart,
The magic of living from a playful heart.
In the tapestry woven, our joys interlace,
The color of laughter brings smiles to each face.

Stories Spun in Sunshine

In golden fields, we sit and dream,
Tales of wonder, flowing like a stream.
Sunshine whispers secrets, bright and clear,
Crafting stories we hold dear.

Laughter dances on the gentle breeze,
As memories twist among the trees.
Each moment shines with laughter's gleam,
In the tapestry of our shared dream.

With every heartbeat, a story unfolds,
Adventures woven with shimmering golds.
We spin our yarns beneath the sky,
In the warmth of sunshine, we soar high.

Colors blaze in the fading light,
Painting tales that take flight.
Each chapter written with love's embrace,
In the sun's glow, we find our place.

So let the stories never cease,
In sunshine's glow, we find our peace.
Together, we'll forge each vibrant line,
In this world where our hearts align.

The Spirit of Playful Adventures

In the heart of the forest, where wonders await,
Footsteps echo, quickening fate.
With laughter and joy as our guiding light,
We dance through the day, chasing the night.

Splashing in puddles, we leap and bound,
Finding magic in each little sound.
The spirit of play whispers soft in our ears,
Chasing away all of our fears.

With each little treasure, a new thrill we find,
In moments of mischief, we leave cares behind.
Soaring on swings, we touch the sky,
In this realm of laughter, we learn to fly.

Under the stars, our stories ignite,
Embracing the wonder, holding on tight.
Every adventure a tale to unfold,
In the spirit of play, we are bold.

Hand in hand, our laughter we share,
In the joyful adventures, life's sweetest care.
With hearts open wide, we roam and explore,
In the spirit of play, we always want more.

Frolics Under a Wide-open Sky

Under the expanse where the horizon lies,
We dance with the clouds, painting the skies.
Frolics arise in the summer's sweet shade,
Where laughter rings out and worries soon fade.

With the sun as our canvas, hearts free to roam,
Every moment we spend feels just like home.
Running in meadows, our spirits take flight,
In the embrace of the warm sunlight.

Kites high above, weaving dreams so bright,
Carried by winds, they take joyful flight.
We spin in circles, lost in delight,
In the tapestry of the day turning night.

With laughter and whispers, we share our tales,
Explorers of wonder, where friendship never fails.
Under the vastness, our hopes intertwine,
In these frolics we cherish, our hearts align.

As the stars emerge, we gather our dreams,
Under a blanket of night, life gleams.
In the joy of the moment, we softly sigh,
Forever enchanted under the wide-open sky.

The Giggles that Bridge Worlds

In the realm of laughter where magic takes flight,
Giggles can shimmer like stars in the night.
They bridge distant lands, connecting us whole,
In a dance of joy that inspires the soul.

Whispers of giggles drape shadows in light,
Turning moments of gloom into sheer delight.
With every chuckle, we weave a new thread,
Creating connections where kindness is spread.

From gardens of dreams to the shores of the sea,
The giggles unite every you and me.
We paint the world bright with smiles and cheer,
In the symphony of love, we draw ever near.

In the laughter's embrace, we find our way through,
Every chuckle a promise, binding me and you.
With hearts intertwined, we share in the joy,
In a world spun from magic, there's no room for coy.

So let the giggles ring out across the lands,
Uniting all souls with warm, gentle hands.
In laughter's sweet chorus, we find our true home,
In the giggles that bridge worlds, together we roam.

The Uplift of Lighthearted Journeys

With laughter echoing through the air,
We wander paths without a care.
The sun ignites each joyful heart,
As friendships bloom, we make our start.

Each step unfolds a brand new dream,
We dance and twirl, our spirits beam.
With every mile, our worries fade,
In light we find the bonds we've made.

Through fields of gold and skies so blue,
We revel in the world anew.
With lightness guiding every turn,
In every heart, the joys we learn.

The laughter lifts, it knows no bounds,
In every echo, bliss abounds.
Together we embrace the day,
As lighthearted moments lead the way.

Serenade of Shared Grins

In the garden where our laughter plays,
We share our secrets, count the days.
A glance, a smile, a joyful wink,
These precious moments link and sync.

As shadows stretch and sunlight glows,
We bask in tales that friendship sows.
Each shared grin writes a story bright,
Creating tunes of pure delight.

With melodies of joy so sweet,
Our hearts compose a rhythmic beat.
In every glance, a spark ignites,
Together shining through the nights.

In gentle breezes, laughs resound,
In this serenade, love is found.
Hand in hand, we face the day,
With shared grins guiding our bright way.

Breezes of Happiness

Whispers of joy on the morning breeze,
Bring smiles and warmth, putting hearts at ease.
With every rustle of the leaves above,
Nature sings softly, reminding us of love.

Through meadows bright and skies so clear,
The breezes carry all we hold dear.
They dance with the laughter, swirl with delight,
A precious canvas painted in light.

In moments fleeting, we lift our gaze,
To endless skies in a joyful haze.
Boundless happiness flows with the air,
In every heartbeat, we're always aware.

Breezes of life guide our way anew,
With whispers of joy that feel so true.
Together we savor this wondrous ride,
In happiness found, we forever abide.

The Journey of Uproarious Tales

Gather 'round for stories grand,
Of laughter shared and dreams unplanned.
With every tale, the room ignites,
We soar on wings of pure delight.

Through mischief, mayhem, and happy cries,
Our spirits lift, we claim the skies.
With each uproarious twist and turn,
The fire of memories brightly burns.

Adventures crafted in laughter's glow,
We chase the magic; we won't let go.
From silly mishaps to wild surprise,
Together, we weave these joyful ties.

As time marches on, we gather near,
Sharing these tales that draw us here.
In every chuckle, a thread we spin,
In this tapestry, we all begin.

Radiant Chuckles Beyond the Mountains

Laughter echoes in the air,
Peaks adorned with joy so rare.
Sunlit faces, grinning wide,
Nature's beauty, our delight.

Meadows sway with playful cheer,
Whispered tales that all can hear.
Clouds above begin to play,
Colors brightening the day.

Streams cascade with giggles sweet,
Every step, a joyful beat.
Mountains witness our embrace,
In this bright and wondrous place.

Breezes carry teasing sounds,
Lively echoes all around.
Footprints left on sodden ground,
In this bliss, we are unbound.

Underneath the twinkling stars,
Dreams take flight, reaching afar.
Radiant chuckles fill the night,
In our hearts, purest light.

The Melody of Mirthful Journeys

On winding roads, we find our tune,
Beneath the sun and glowing moon.
With every mile, our laughter swells,
In every heart, a story dwells.

Songs of joy, they lead the way,
Through valleys lush and bright array.
With friends beside, the world is vast,
Each joyful moment, never passed.

Chasing dreams on rustling leaves,
Unfolding tales, our mind achieves.
Winding paths like rivers flow,
With every step, our spirits grow.

Whispers of the breeze so light,
Guide our hearts, ignite the night.
In every laugh, a lingering song,
Together here, we all belong.

The melody of life inspires,
A symphony that never tires.
In every journey, mirth we find,
As joy and laughter intertwine.

Glee's Voyage through Time and Space

Across the stars, we sail so free,
Time and space our company.
With glee as our guiding star,
We travel near and wander far.

Galaxies twinkle, laughter bright,
In cosmic games, we share delight.
Each moment, a spark in the night,
Together we dance, hearts alight.

Echoes of joy in the voids we find,
Adventure awaits for those inclined.
Through nebulae, we chase the light,
Infinite journeys take flight.

An astral carousel, spinning around,
In the boundless skies, glee is found.
With each heartbeat, time unwinds,
Eternal laughter, true love binds.

With every star, a memory we make,
A timeless voyage, never to break.
Glee's laughter, a radiant show,
Together we wander, forever we glow.

Jests that Dance on the Waves

On rolling tides, our laughs arise,
Bright jests beneath the sunny skies.
With every splash, a cheer that's shared,
The ocean's song, our hearts laid bare.

Seagulls join in with playful flights,
In the salty air, our spirits ignite.
Wave by wave, we play, we glide,
Nature's whimsy as our guide.

Tales unfold on sandy shores,
With playful waves that crack and roar.
Each echo brings the past to light,
In laughter, all our fears take flight.

Underneath the sun's warm glow,
Jests that dance and ebb and flow.
Together we chase the horizon wide,
In each heartbeat, joy is our ride.

The ocean's laughter, a timeless tune,
Rising high under the glowing moon.
In every wave, a memory plays,
Jests forever, in joyous waves.

Echoes of Joyful Whispers

In the garden of soft dreams,
Laughter dances on the breeze,
Petals flutter, sunlight beams,
Hope awakens with such ease.

Children play under the trees,
Voices blend like sweet perfume,
Joyful whispers ride the leaves,
Bringing life to every room.

Memory's glow, a tender spark,
Reflecting in each gleaming eye,
In shadows deep, in bright and dark,
We find the love that will not die.

Painted skies in colors bold,
Promises wrapped in every hue,
Stories whispered, tales retold,
In every heart, a song rings true.

So let the echoes softly sing,
A symphony of laughter bright,
In every moment, joy will spring,
As whispers lead us to the light.

Beyond the Boundless Giggle

Laughter bubbles, light as air,
Chasing shadows, bright and free,
With every giggle, joy to share,
Together we can always be.

Clouds drift by, a playful sight,
As we leap with hearts in sync,
Beyond the stars, beyond the night,
In dreams we swim, in colors pink.

Silver linings grace the day,
With every smile, the world will bloom,
Casting worries far away,
In the warmth, there's always room.

We dance in circles, spinning round,
Echoes of laughter fill the air,
In this paradise we have found,
Love surrounds us everywhere.

Hold this moment, let it stay,
In the tender light of dawn,
From boundless giggles, joy will play,
As we carry on and on.

Chasing Sunbeams of Delight

Chasing sunbeams, bright and bold,
In fields where laughter starts to grow,
Every ray, a wish untold,
In their glow, our spirits flow.

Golden moments weave the day,
As shadows dance in playful chase,
Through whispered dreams, we find our way,
In sunlight's arms, we find our place.

Joyfully, we run and leap,
With hands outstretched to greet the sky,
In this dance, our hearts will keep,
The sweetness of a carefree sigh.

Each sunbeam holds a memory,
Of laughter shared beneath the trees,
In every glance, a melody,
Of friendship's love and summer's ease.

Hold the light, let spirits soar,
Chasing wonders, hearts ignite,
In the warmth, we crave for more,
For sunbeams spark our pure delight.

Melodies of Mirth in the Sky

In the twilight, soft and sweet,
Melodies drift on the breeze,
Voices of mirth, a playful beat,
Carried through the rustling leaves.

Stars awaken, twinkle bright,
Dancing to the rhythm of night,
With every note, our spirits raise,
In laughter's glow, we find our ways.

To the sky, our dreams take flight,
As joy entwines with heaven's song,
In the silence, pure delight,
Whispers echo, soft and strong.

Together, we will chase the glow,
With every harmony that we find,
In this melody, love will flow,
Binding hearts and souls entwined.

So let the night be filled with cheer,
Melodies of mirth fill the air,
In every laugh, we hold so dear,
Together, joy is everywhere.

Celebrations Above the Clouds

Balloons rise high in bright azure skies,
Laughter echoes as the sunshine flies.
Dancing on air, spirits soar so free,
Whispers of joy, a sweet symphony.

Fireworks bloom in a vibrant display,
Colors burst forth, igniting the day.
Friends gather close with smiles all around,
In this warm moment, true love is found.

Songs of the heart drift on gentle winds,
Embracing the light, where happiness begins.
Every cheer woven, a tapestry bright,
Under the heavens, we bask in the light.

As twilight descends, stars start to gleam,
Dreams take flight in a harmonious stream.
Together we dance, lost in delight,
Celebrations above, a magical night.

The Bridge of Happy Voices

A bridge spans wide, connecting each heart,
Laughter and joy are where friendships start.
Voices unite in a melodious song,
Together we feel we truly belong.

Stories unfold in the warm evening glow,
Sharing our hopes, letting our spirits flow.
Magnificent tales of both old and new,
Carved in our memories, ever true.

Children's laughter dances in the air,
Echoing dreams without a single care.
The rhythm of life beats strong and alive,
On this bridge of voices, we all thrive.

When shadows fall, and stars start to shine,
We gather together, our spirits align.
Hand in hand, with hearts open wide,
On this bridge of joy, we take our stride.

Echoes of Playfulness in Every Breeze

Gentle whispers ride on the wings of the night,
Echoes of laughter that fill up the light.
Children at play, their giggles abound,
In every soft rustle, pure joy can be found.

Daisies and butterflies dance in the sun,
Moments of magic, where time seems to run.
With hearts unburdened, we cherish the ray,
Embracing the wonder that brightens our day.

Every breeze carries a sprinkle of cheer,
A melody sweet that we hold so dear.
With each playful twist that nature does weave,
We find our delight in what we believe.

As day fades softly, and stars take their place,
We gather our dreams, with love we embrace.
In echoes of play, we find our release,
In every breeze whispers the gift of peace.

Harmonics of Joy in the Distance

In the distance, melodies sway with the trees,
Harmonics of joy float softly on the breeze.
Notes of connection drift through the air,
Binding our hearts in a moment so rare.

Golden rays spill as the sun starts to set,
Filling our souls with no hint of regret.
Every glance shared ignites warmth from within,
In this sweet symphony, together we spin.

Waves of sweet laughter arise from the ground,
As life dances lightly, spinning around.
With rhythms that pulse, and echoes that gleam,
Joy blossoms softly, like a radiant dream.

In the hush of the night, stars begin to sing,
Harmonies rich, all the beauty they bring.
Together we gather through shadows and light,
In the distance, joy finds us tonight.

Grins that Travel the World

A smile can cross the seas,
In every land, it brings some ease.
From city streets to mountain peaks,
A simple grin, the heart it seeks.

Across the plains and through the trees,
Laughter dances with the breeze.
In every culture, every face,
A joy that time cannot erase.

Sunrise beams on bustling streets,
In every heart, a rhythm beats.
With open arms, we share our light,
Grins that travel, pure delight.

Under starlit skies so wide,
With every smile, we bridge the tide.
Uniting souls from far and near,
Through grins, we lessen every fear.

So let the world embrace this bliss,
With every frown, we find the kiss.
In journeys bold, our spirits twirl,
With grins that travel all the world.

A Symphony of Joyful Whispers

In quiet corners, laughter sighs,
A melody beneath the skies.
Soft notes of joy weave through the air,
Each whisper carries love and care.

With every twinkle, every glance,
Moments play their sweet romance.
A symphony of gentle cheer,
With open hearts, we hold them near.

The rustle of the autumn leaves,
In whispered tones, our spirit weaves.
An orchestra of dreams ignites,
In every soul, a spark of light.

The pitter-patter of feet in dance,
Life's warm embrace in every chance.
Together, we compose the score,
In unison, we seek for more.

So let the world embrace the sound,
In every heartbeat, joy is found.
A symphony we share, it's clear,
With joyful whispers, we draw near.

Breezy Tales of Delight

A breeze that whispers through the trees,
Carries tales with gentle ease.
From blooming fields to ocean waves,
Each story danced, the heart it saves.

With every gust, a laugh takes flight,
Breezy tales in soft sunlight.
They weave through moments, light and bright,
In every smile, a spark ignites.

The stories told in friendships grown,
In laughter shared, we are not alone.
A tapestry of all our dreams,
In breezy tales, the spirit beams.

As seasons change, so too does cheer,
In breezy tales, the path is clear.
With open hearts, we dare to roam,
In every tale, we find our home.

So let the breezes softly call,
In whispered tales, we rise, we fall.
United in our quests of light,
With breezy tales of pure delight.

The Universal Language of Joy

Across the globe, a laughter rings,
It dances lightly on the wings.
In every heart, a feeling grows,
The universal joy that flows.

From mountain tops to oceans deep,
In every culture, secrets keep.
Yet through it all, a bond we share,
In joyful moments, truth laid bare.

With every smile, a bridge we build,
Connections formed, our hearts are filled.
In gentle nods and shared delight,
The language spoken feels so right.

As children laugh and neighbors play,
The world ignites in bright array.
With every touch, we come alive,
In joy, the human spirit thrives.

So let us speak this language true,
In every dawn, in every hue.
Together bound, we find our way,
In joy's embrace, we choose to stay.

The Voyage of Cheerful Encounters

In the gentle breeze they sail,
With laughter echoing on the trail.
Every wave a song they sing,
On this joyous voyage, hearts take wing.

Bright horizons call the day,
As dreams and wonders light the way.
Friendship beams like the sun above,
Guiding them through realms of love.

Nights are filled with stars that dance,
Each twinkle sparks a new romance.
With every port, a tale to tell,
Of cheerful encounters cast so well.

The colors of the sunset blaze,
As laughter warms the evening haze.
They share their hopes, their dreams unwound,
In every moment, joy is found.

So raise a glass to those who roam,
In search of laughter, finding home.
The voyage continues, ever bright,
With cheerful hearts and spirits light.

Festive Gales of Merriment

In the field where laughter plays,
Joyful hearts weave through the maze.
Colorful banners flap in cheer,
As festive gales draw friends near.

Dancing shadows prance and sway,
With every beat, they chase dismay.
Music flows like summer dew,
Uniting souls in laughter true.

Firelight glows against the night,
Whispers shared by soft moonlight.
In every story, joy is spun,
Merriment shines when day is done.

Cupcakes piled, the feast begins,
With stolen bites and cheeky grins.
Together they savor each delight,
In this festival, hearts are light.

As night turns into dawn anew,
Memories forged in shades of blue.
A tapestry of joy displayed,
In festive gales, all worries fade.

Chronicles of Bubbly Revelry

In the hall where laughter rings,
Bubbly hearts flutter like wings.
Every toast a tale unfolds,
In chronicle of joy retold.

With sparkling eyes and endless cheer,
They dance through moments, year by year.
Champagne bubbles rise and pop,
Each sip a promise, never stop.

As stories blend with laughter bright,
They weave a tapestry of light.
In every wink, in every smile,
Bubbly revelry spans a mile.

The clock strikes hours lost in song,
Where every spirit, bold, belongs.
Together they soar, hearts entwined,
In blissful revelry, peace combined.

Remembered moments linger on,
In chronicles where all are drawn.
With every hug, the night is sealed,
In bubbly joy, their fates revealed.

Tumbling Tales of Delight

Through valleys green where laughter flows,
Tumbling tales, as friendship grows.
In every corner, joy is spun,
Delightful moments, never done.

Chasing shadows, bright and bold,
Stories shimmer, secrets told.
With every step, adventure calls,
In tumbling tales, the spirit sprawls.

Beneath the stars, they share their dreams,
Whispers drift on moonlit beams.
With a flick of fate, a spark ignites,
Tumbling stories into the nights.

As dawn awakes, they gather round,
In the warmth of joy profound.
Each laughter shared, a thread so bright,
In tumbling tales, hearts take flight.

So let them dance, let voices rise,
In every smile, a new surprise.
With each delight, their spirits soar,
In tumbling tales, forevermore.

A Carousel of Smiles

Round and round, the colors play,
Laughter bubbles, bright as day.
Each face gleams with pure delight,
As happiness takes flight.

Every spin, a memory spun,
A dance of joy, we all are one.
In swirling lights, we lose our cares,
In this moment, love declares.

The music plays, the world stands still,
Chasing glee, a timeless thrill.
Hands reach out, we touch the sky,
In this place, we learn to fly.

Grinning wide, our hearts aligned,
In this ride, true peace we find.
Round and round, a joyful chase,
In a carousel, we embrace.

So gather close, let laughter soar,
In this dance, we crave for more.
With every turn, let our hearts beam,
On this carousel, we dream.

The Exuberance of the Open Sky

Up above, so vast and wide,
Clouds drift lazily, side by side.
Golden rays break through the grey,
Chasing shadows far away.

Birds take flight, a joyful scene,
In the blue, they dance serene.
Every breeze, a whispered song,
In the sky, where we belong.

Mountains high and valleys deep,
Nature's wonders, ours to keep.
With open hearts, we reach the light,
In this expanse, dreams take flight.

Stars emerge as day is done,
Secret stories, every one.
In endless night, the world aglow,
Boundless beauty, always flows.

Exuberance in every hue,
The open sky, a canvas new.
We paint our hopes, we sing our dreams,
In this realm, nothing redeems.

Serenades from Distant Shores

Melodies drift upon the breeze,
Carried far across the seas.
Softly sung by distant choirs,
Igniting hearts like hidden fires.

Waves respond with rhythmic dance,
In the moonlight, we take a chance.
With every note, our spirits rise,
In these serenades, we find the skies.

Whispers of the ocean's call,
Echo in the night, enthrall.
Stories told of love and lore,
From distant lands, we yearn for more.

Sailing dreams on gentle tides,
In harmony, our heart resides.
Voices blend, as one they sing,
In these songs, our souls take wing.

Every note, a treasure sought,
In distant shores, we find what's taught.
Serenades that never fade,
In their arms, our fears are laid.

The Endless Cycle of Joyful Memories

Time spins round, a constant wheel,
Memories crafted, hearts they heal.
Each moment shared, a gentle kiss,
In the cycle, we find our bliss.

Laughing faces, friends held dear,
Echoes of love, always near.
Through seasons change, our bonds grow tight,
In the endless flow, we find the light.

From whispered dreams to laughter loud,
In every memory, we feel proud.
Though time may fade, the love stays clear,
In every story, we hold dear.

Year by year, we build our nest,
In joyful times, we find our rest.
The cycle turns, and still we cling,
To every memory, life's sweet song we sing.

So let us gather, hand in hand,
In this dance, forever stand.
The endless cycle spins anew,
With joyful memories, we'll push through.

Festooning the World with Cheer

Banners flutter in the breeze,
Colors burst like blooms in spring.
Joyful hearts sing melodies,
In every corner, laughter rings.

Children dance beneath bright skies,
Faces lit with pure delight.
Gifts of kindness, sweet surprise,
Sharing warmth, igniting light.

From every place, a story shared,
With every smile, hope unfurls.
United we stand, hearts laid bare,
Festooning the world with cheer.

In the glow of twilight's grace,
Magic lingers in the air.
Together we find our place,
A tapestry, free from care.

So let us weave a vibrant thread,
With love and joy as our guide.
In every heart, let dreams be bred,
Festooning life with hearts wide.

Whimsical Winds of Togetherness

Under the stars, we gather near,
The whimsical winds, they call our name.
Echoing laughter, transcending fear,
Together, we rise in friendship's flame.

Gentle whispers dance through trees,
Carrying tales of hearts entwined.
On this journey, we sail with ease,
In unity, our souls aligned.

Every moment, a treasure sought,
Shared dreams float like leaves in the air.
With every word, a bond is wrought,
In this haven, love sings fair.

As sunrays weave through morning mist,
We chase the dawn on open seas.
Hand in hand, none shall be missed,
Whimsical winds, our hearts at ease.

Together we brave life's winding ride,
With hope's compass, we steer the way.
In laughter, our spirits abide,
Whimsical winds lead us each day.

Traces of Grins Across Seas

Footprints left on sandy shores,
Across the tides, our laughter flows.
With every wave, a memory roars,
Traces of grins where friendship grows.

Beneath the sun's warm embrace,
Connections span both land and tide.
In every heart, a special place,
Togetherness, our faithful guide.

We write our tales in the breeze,
Letters drift on currents strong.
Every moment, a sweet reprise,
In harmony, we all belong.

Across the seas, we hope to find,
A bridge of smiles that never fades.
In shadows cast, love stays aligned,
Traces of grins, our joyful shades.

So let us sail with open dreams,
On waves of cheer, forever bold.
In every heart, a dance that gleams,
Traces of grins, a story told.

Bridges Built with Glee

With every step, we bridge the gap,
Hand in hand, we find our way.
Joyful hearts hold every map,
Building dreams where skies are gray.

From laughter shared to tears embraced,
Every moment, a brighter hue.
In every challenge, hope replaced,
Together, we'll always break through.

The paths we forge through fields of gold,
Each memory a treasured key.
With stories whispered, stories bold,
Bridges built with glee, you see.

Through every storm, we stand as one,
With love as our perpetual guide.
Underneath the warming sun,
The strength of joy will not subside.

So let us gather, souls in flight,
Creating bridges, vast and free.
In every heart, a spark of light,
Together we build with glee.

Sun-kissed Bubbles of Joy

In the morning light we play,
Chasing dreams that float away,
With laughter sweet and hearts so free,
Sun-kissed bubbles dance with glee.

Joyful spirits rise and spin,
Whispers soft, where love begins,
Each moment glows, a treasure found,
In every smile, our hearts abound.

Children's giggles fill the air,
As we twirl without a care,
Floating high on hopes so bright,
Underneath the golden light.

Every bubble's burst brings cheer,
Memories made, forever near,
Caught in laughter, never shy,
Sun-kissed bubbles fly up high.

In the dusk, we pause and beam,
Relishing our painted dream,
Each bubble glimmers, glows with grace,
In our hearts, their sweet embrace.

Journeys Wrapped in Laughter

Footsteps echo on the trail,
Stories shared, we will not fail,
In every twist, a smile appears,
Journeys wrapped in laughter's cheers.

Winding roads and skies so wide,
Hand in hand, we take the ride,
With playful jests, our worries cease,
In joyful moments, we find peace.

Through fields of green and skies of blue,
We share our hearts, our dreams anew,
With every step, the joy we find,
A journey cherished, souls aligned.

As sunsets paint the world in gold,
Memories of laughter unfold,
In every chuckle, every song,
Together's where we all belong.

Under starlit skies so bright,
We share our hopes, our pure delight,
In bonds of laughter, our spirits thrive,
On this journey, we come alive.

The Tapestry of Joyful Echoes

Each thread we weave a tale to spin,
Moments bright where love begins,
In the colors of our shared delight,
The tapestry glows, a wondrous sight.

Whispers soft as breezes flow,
Stories told in vibrant glow,
As laughter dances through the night,
Echoes of joy take joyful flight.

With every stitch, a memory made,
In threads of gold, our dreams cascade,
Intertwined with warmth and care,
A tapestry rich beyond compare.

From laughter's depths, our spirits rise,
In the fabric of love, the ties,
We craft a world where happiness thrives,
In joyful echoes, our heart survives.

The nights may fade, but we remain,
Woven together through joy and pain,
In every hue, our story will show,
The tapestry shines with warmth aglow.

Glimmers of Happiness on the Horizon

With every dawn, the world awakes,
Sunlight breaking, shadow shakes,
Glimmers dance on morning's dew,
Happiness whispers, fresh and new.

In laughter's song, the heart takes flight,
Painting dreams in colors bright,
On horizons wide, we seek to find,
A world of joy that's intertwined.

Every challenge fades with a smile,
Steps of hope stretch every mile,
With glimmers guiding us ahead,
We walk the path where joy is bred.

As starlit nights bring peace so bold,
Stories of happiness unfold,
In every twinkle, light shines clear,
A promise kept, our dreams endear.

Together we chase the setting sun,
With laughter shared, our hearts as one,
Glimmers of joy, forever bright,
On the horizon, pure delight.

The Spirit of Joyful Union

In laughter's embrace we find our place,
With every smile, a warm trace.
Hearts entwined through thick and thin,
In joyful union, we begin.

Hands held tight in the dance of time,
Every moment feels like a rhyme.
As sunlight breaks the dawn anew,
Our spirits soar, united, too.

Through trials faced and dreams we weave,
Together we conquer, yes, believe.
In this bond, our worries stray,
The spirit of union lights the way.

With whispers soft and laughter loud,
Together we stand, forever proud.
Through storms and sun, we chart our course,
Love ignites a boundless force.

Amidst the chaos, still we shine,
In joyful union, hearts align.
A tapestry crafted, rich and bright,
With threads of joy woven tight.

Skylines Painted with Jests

Beneath wide skies of azure hue,
Laughter dances, bold and true.
With every jest, our spirits soar,
As dreams build high, we seek for more.

The sun sets low, a canvas bright,
Colors blend in fading light.
Each chuckle paints a stroke divine,
Skylines glow, like stars they shine.

In bustling streets where stories blend,
Humor whispers, hearts transcend.
A playful banter, joy released,
In the skyline, laughter feasts.

With every wink, a bond we share,
In this city, joy is rare.
Tales of mirth are passed along,
In jest and cheer, we all belong.

So let us lift our voices high,
Underneath that painted sky.
With laughter's brush, our hearts ignite,
In every jest, we find our light.

Vibrations of Good Humor

In the melody of joy we sway,
Laughter rings like bells at play.
With every chuckle, hearts combine,
In good humor's glow, we shine.

Through tales of folly, smiles arise,
A symphony beneath the skies.
Each burst of laughter, pure and free,
Vibrations of joy, you and me.

With jest and jive, we take our stand,
In every wink, a helping hand.
United in this joyful tune,
Our spirits sway like the afternoon.

Through ups and downs, we rise and fall,
In good humor, we embrace it all.
A chorus sung with hearts so bold,
In these vibrations, stories unfold.

So let us dance to laughter's song,
With every jest, we all belong.
Together weaving, hearts entwined,
In good humor, love defined.

Heartstrings Plucked by Delight

In gentle breezes, joy takes flight,
Heartstrings plucked with pure delight.
With every smile that lights the way,
We find our hope in a brand new day.

A touch of magic fills the air,
In laughter shared, burdens we bear.
With each sweet note, our spirits rise,
In melodies that harmonize.

Through whispered dreams and playful cheer,
Delight ignites when friends are near.
In moments grasped, like shimmering dew,
Our hearts resonate, strong and true.

As day turns dusk, our laughter glows,
In the warmth of friendship, true love flows.
Heartstrings dance in a joyous light,
In every heartbeat, pure delight.

So let us cherish what we find,
In laughter's arms, we're intertwined.
With every chuckle, joy ignites,
In this symphony of pure delights.

The Map of Joyful Connections

In every corner, hearts align,
A tapestry of love entwined.
With laughter shared, and hopes that soar,
We trace the paths, forevermore.

In whispers soft, our dreams unfold,
A story new, yet ages old.
Through endless bonds and moments bright,
We find our way in pure delight.

Through valleys deep, by rivers wide,
With kindred spirits by our side.
We navigate with open hearts,
Discovering joy in every part.

As laughter rings and shadows fade,
Our friendships bloom, never betrayed.
In every journey, twists and bends,
The map of joy, where love transcends.

United souls, we dance as one,
Under the sun, 'til day is done.
With every step, we forge anew,
A vibrant path; a bond so true.

Fountains of Laughter Under the Stars

In twilight's glow, our spirits rise,
As laughter spills beneath the skies.
With every splash, we feel alive,
In fountains bright where joy will thrive.

The moonlit dance, a joyful spree,
With friends beside, we're wild and free.
Each giggle soft, like whispers rare,
A symphony of love laid bare.

Fountains flow with memories sweet,
In every heart, the rhythm beats.
Under the stars, our dreams take flight,
A boundless joy that feels so right.

As shadows play, the night unfolds,
A canvas bright with tales retold.
We share our hopes, our secrets dear,
In laughter's arms, we conquer fear.

With every splash, our spirits soar,
In laughter's grip, we crave for more.
Together we find, in every glance,
A universe of joy, a dance.

The Troupe of Merriment

Gathered close, the troupe convenes,
Where smiles arise, and joy intervenes.
We paint the world with colors bright,
In every moment, pure delight.

Through jokes and jests, we lift our cheer,
A circle wide, with laughter near.
In every heart, a candle glows,
The warmth of friendship, ever grows.

With every act, a tale unfolds,
The magic shared, a joy retold.
In rhythms free, we twirl and spin,
Together still, as love flows in.

From silly games to heartfelt tunes,
We dance beneath the silver moons.
Each giggle shared, a thread of gold,
In every heart, our tales are told.

In merriment, we find our grace,
A family bound in joy's embrace.
With every cheer, we paint the day,
The troupe of life, forever play.

Effervescent Echoes Across the Globe

In cities bright, where laughter rings,
The echoes dance on friendly wings.
Across the globe, a bond we share,
Effervescent joy fills the air.

From mountain tops to ocean shores,
With open hearts, we seek for more.
Each voice a note, a melody,
Together weaving harmony.

In laughter's glow, we find our way,
Through every night and shining day.
From every land, a story told,
In echoes bright, our dreams unfold.

United still, though miles apart,
In every beat, we blend one heart.
The world a stage, we rise and shine,
With every smile, the stars align.

In every corner, joy we spark,
With friendships formed, we leave a mark.
Effervescent echoes, loud and clear,
A symphony of love held dear.